DREAM FOR UDAYACHAL

BY PTCA

Contents

Dream For Udayachal

BY PTCA

I

Introduction

On 27th February 1967, the Plains Tribal Council of Assam (PTCA) was born under the leadership of SAMAR BRAHMA CHOUDHURY and CHARAN NARZARY in the political field of Assam. The founder president of the PTCA was BIRUSAN DOLEY and CHARAN NARZARY was the founder secretary.

The year 1967 was the most important in the political history of Assam. Because the announcement of the then PRIME MINISTER INDIRA GANDHI where she announced that Assam will be re-organised on federal basis on 13th January 1967.

II

Demand for Udayachal

The PTCA demanded for the creation of Union Territory in the name of "UDAYACHAL". The demand for "UDAYACHAL" got a massive support from the Plains Tribal people where they were predominant.

The second meeting of the PTCA was held at EDENBARI (DARRANG DISTRICT) on 8th April 1967 and took many decisions. The meeting also decided to publish a weekly news magazine in the name and style of the "JANAJATI" as an organ of the PTCA for inspiring the people politically, socially and economically. The territory of UDAYACHAL is sought to be created by clubbing the predominantly Plains Tribal area of northern tracts of the river Brahmaputra along the foot hills of Bhutan and Arunachal. When the then Prime Minister Indira Gandhi came to Assam on 10th March 1983, the leaders of the PTCA met her and demanded the creation of "UDAYACHAL".

After the meeting, then Prime Minister Indira Gandhi advised the leaders of the PTCA to prepare and submit the geographical justification of their demand. Accordingly, a team of the PTCA led by Samar Brahma Chaudhury, Charan Narzary and few other leaders submitted necessary papers to the Prime Minister relating to the geographical feasibility of their demand for the creation of Udayachal on 17th May 1983. Copy of documents was submitted to the Special HOME SECRETARY, MR. P. P. NAYER AND THE CABINET SECRETARY, GOVERNMENT OF INDIA, MR. KRISHNA SWAMY RAO SAHEB.

In relation to the demand for UDAYACHAL, a delegation team of the PTCA met the then Prime Minister Rajib Gandhi on 29th April 1986 and urged to solve their demand. On 27.09.86, a four member PTCA delegation led by Shri Samar Brahma Choudhury, M.P., met the union HOME MINISTER SHRI BUTA SING and reiterated the urgent need to create the proposed union territory of Udayachal. On the basis of the discussion, then Home Minister called for a tripartite talk between the Central Government, State Government and the leaders of the PTCA on the demand for the creation of Union Territory.

III
Splits in PTCA

In the following year i.e. 1977, PTCA had changed their demand from 'UNION TERRITORY' TO 'AUTONOMOUS REGION'. After they change of their demand from 'Union Territory' to 'Autonomous Region' a section of the PTCA workers did not support that demand and ultimately this was a split of the party and formed a new political party named as PLAINS TRIBAL COUNCIL OF ASSAM (PROGRESSIVE) (PTCA-P) on 22nd May 1978 under the leadership of BINOY KUMAR BASUMATARI. The main demand of the PTCA-P was the creation of a 'MISING BODOLAND'. For the creation of a 'MISSING BODOLAND' the PTCA-P submitted a memorandum to then Prime Minister Indira Gandhi on 8th July 1980.

To create regional autonomy for the Bodos, another political party was emerged in the month of April 1984 named as UNITED TRIBAL NATIONALIST LIBERATION FRONT (UTNLF). The UTNLF demanded Union Territory which was known as 'TRIBAL LAND'. For that the party submitted a memorandum to the then Prime Minister Rajib Gandhi on 12th March 1986. But the UTNLF also did not survive for long time and a portion of the party workers formed another party which was known as the UNITED BODO NATIONALIST LIBERATION FRONT (UBNLF).

IV

Bodo Movement under Plains Tribal Council of Assam (PTCA)

The Bodo movement prior to 1967 was mostly non-political in nature. Much of the activities of the movement were limited to petitions, prayers and memorandums. The emphasis of the movement was on socio-religious reforms and economic upliftment of the Bodos. Even though political aspirations of the plains tribal found expression during this period, it was only for the fulfillment of some specific demand and representation in the law making bodies. However, there has come a qualitative change in the nature of movement in 1967. On 13th January 1967, Mrs. Indira Gandhi announced the Government of India's proposal to reorganize Assam in order to meet the demand of All Party Hill Leaders Conference (APHLC) for a separate hill state. This decision of the Government of India was widely appreciated by the tribals of Assam. In response to this declaration, All Bodo Students' Union (ABSU) was formed on 15th February 1967 at Kokrajhar Tribal Rest House. Similarly, on 27th February 1967, the Plains Tribal Council of Assam (PTCA) was formed. Both ABSU and PTCA warmly welcomed the policy of reorganizing Assam. On 9th June 1967, a five-member delegation of PTCA met the PRESIDENT OF INDIA DR. ZAKIR HUSAIN at Rastrapati Bhawan and submitted their first memorandum dated on 20th May 1967. In course of their meeting with the President, PTCA delegation explained the miserable plight of the plains tribals in Assam and demanded full autonomy in the tribal inhabited areas comprising the northern tracts of Goalpara, Kamrup, Darrang, Lakhimpur and Sibsagar district along the foothills of Bhutan and North East Frontier Tracts (present Arunachal Pradesh). On 10th June 1967, the delegation met the Union Home Minister Mr. Y. V. Chavan and Union Industries Development Minister MR. FAKHRUDDIN ALI AHMED and handed over the copies of their memorandum to them. The memorandum runs "The Plains Tribals Council of Assam deems that full autonomy within the framework of the Indian Constitution will alone help the plains tribals grow according to their own genius and tradition. The plains tribal people of Assam have since long been demanding full autonomy comprising the predominantly tribal inhabited areas of plains Assam" (Memorandum submitted to the PRESIDENT OF INDIA BY PTCA ON 20TH MAY 1967). Initially, no nomenclature was given to the proposed autonomous plains tribal region. But with a view to give a rough idea about the proposed tribal region, a map was prepared by PTCA which extends from the river Sankosh in the West to Sadiya in the East along the foothills of Bhutan and the North Eastern Frontier Tracts on the northern part of river Brahmaputra. Expressing their grave concerns over the problems of land alienation of the tribals in Assam PTCA remarked "The plains tribals are essentially cultivators and agriculture is the mainstay of their economy. Hence, land is of supreme importance to them. But there has been constant attack on tribal lands. Large number of East Bengal immigrants started to pour into tribal areas since the beginning of this century and settled therein. Apart from the East Bengal immigrants, local non-tribal traders, businessmen and money-lenders also have been onslaughting the lands belonging to the tribals. All these forces were constant menace to simple and peace loving plains tribals of Assam" (Memorandum submitted to the President of India by PTCA on 20th May 1967). PTCA also considered that the existing constituencies, both Parliament as well as the State Assembly were delimited in such a way that tribals have been made minority even though there was clear cut instructions in the Delimitation of Constituencies Act 1962 to locate the reserved seats for the tribals in such area where the population of the tribals are largest. In protest of such arrangement, PTCA resolved not to participate in any election in future unless all the ST reserved constituencies, whether Parliamentary or Assembly are redelimited as per the instructions of the Delimitation of Constituencies Act 1962. They boycotted the by-election of Kokrajhar Parliamentary Constituency held on 19th May 1968. Thousands of unarmed Bodo people including the other tribals supported the boycott of election called by the PTCA. However, this step of PTCA had to face serious challenges because of the imposition of prohibitory orders. Thousands of PTCA volunteers, both men and women, who picketed the polling stations were arrested and sent to different jails in the state. On 7th January 1973, the demand of proposed autonomous region was upgraded to the demand of 'Union Territory' in the name of 'Udayachal'.

V

Roman Script Movement

However, by 1974, the wave of Roman script movement of Bodos broke out which temporarily slowed down the pace of Udayachal movement. The Roman script movement was launched by Bodo Sahitya Sabha for adoption of Roman Script in writing Bodo language. In this movement, thousands of Bodos participated with great enthusiasm. ABSU also strongly participated in the movement. But the movement was ruthlessly suppressed by the state government and thousands of the Bodo people were put to jail where they suffered inhuman tortures. During this movement, at least15 supporters were shot to death by Assam Police. In the meantime, national emergency was declared in 1975 and the problem of the leaders of the movement increased. The movement for Roman script ended with a surprise outcome with the intervention of the then Prime Minister Mrs. Indira Gandhi. After several rounds of discussion between Bodo leaders and the Government of India, Devnagri script was adopted for alphabet of Bodos. However, the Bodos felt that Central Government along with PTCA leaders imposed Devnagri script upon the unwilling Bodo masses.

VI

PTCA as Political Party

In 1978, PTCA participated jointly with the Janata Party in the Assembly Election where they put their candidates in nine Assembly Constituencies. They joined in the Coalition Ministry formed by Janata Party under the Chief Ministership of Mr. Golap Borbora.

VII
Changes in PTCA's demand

But suddenly, a change was noticed in the nature of the demand of PTCA. On 4th April 1977, PTCA announced that the party had renounced the demand of 'Udayachal' and wants go along the demand of autonomous region. This move of the PTCA leaders created differences within the party which ultimately resulted in split in the party and formation of the PLAINS TRIBAL COUNCIL OF ASSAM (PROGRESSIVE) by the hardliners of the party on 22nd May 1979. This party later on assumed the name of UNITED TRIBAL NATIONALIST LIBERATION FRONT (UTNLF). This move of the PTCA leaders to withdraw their demand for Udayachal was also strongly condemned by ABSU who supported PTCA in their movement for the union territory of Udayachal.

VIII
Conclusion

Finally, as the time rolled, misunderstanding and differences between the Bodo leadership, particularly between PTCA and ABSU increased and subsequently it turned violent. Then there took place number of revenge killings between ABSU and PTCA which seriously disrupted peace in the region. Charan Narzary in his book "Dream for Udayachal and the History of Plains Tribal Council of Assam" has estimated the number of death toll at 249 and said that it does not cover the names of all victims of these internal conflicts as many names of the victims could not be collected during that time. These internal conflicts have also been responsible for the change of guard and decline of PTCA as the leader of the Bodo movement.